BUTTERFLIES ARE FREE

Copyright 2025 Shirley M. Ford
Butterflies Are Free

Published by Yawn's Publishing
2555 Marietta Hwy, Ste 103
Canton, GA 30114
www.yawnsbooks.com

All rights reserved. No part of this book may be reproduced or transmitted in any form, electronic or mechanical, including photocopying, recording, or data storage systems without the express written permission of the publisher, except for brief quotations in reviews and articles.

Library of Congress Control Number: 2025906467

ISBN: 978-1-966815-02-0 paperback
       978-1-966815-04-4 hardcover

The MacArthur Study Bible NASB
New American Standard Updated Edition
All scripture taken from the New American Standard Bible ®, Copyright © 1960, 1962, 1963, 1968, 1971, '72, '73, '75, '77, '95 by the Lochman Foundation. Used by permission.

Printed in the United States

*The butterfly reminds us that life is short
and we have the freedom to enjoy each moment.*

*Through transformation, we change, inspire hope,
endure, have joy, and display courage in difficult times.*

*Like a butterfly, we emerge from our cocoon
and become the paths we choose in life.*

Shirley M. Ford

 # TABLE OF CONTENTS

🦋	A FEW LAUGHS	1
🦋	ENCOURAGEMENT	9
🦋	THE CHILDREN'S HOUR	35
🦋	SOME STORIES	47
🦋	ONE LINERS	63

Shirley Ford

 **A FEW LAUGHS**

Butterflies Are Free

•

Always borrow money from a pessimist.
He won't expect it back.
Oscar Wilde

•

The difference between stupidity and genius
is that genius has its limits.
Albert Einstein

•

Have you ever noticed that anybody driving slower
than you is an idiot, and anyone going faster
than you is a maniac?
George Carlin

•

Here's something to think about:
How come you never see a headline
like "Psychic Wins Lottery?"
Jay Leno

•

Just once, I want a username and
password prompt to say: "CLOSE ENOUGH."
Author Unknown

•

It may be that your sole purpose in life
is simply to serve as a warning to others.
Jill Shalus, Head Over Heels

•

•

Drive carefully.. . . . . . . it's not only cars
that can be recalled by their Maker.
BumperArt.com

•

Almost everything will work again
if you unplug it for a few minutes, including yourself.
Anne Lamont

•

People who think they know everything
are a great annoyance to those of us who do.
Isaac Asmov

•

It takes less time to do a thing right,
than it does to explain why you did it wrong.
Henry Wadsworth Longfellow

•

The road to success is always under construction.
Lily Tomlin

•

THE LETTER

Just a line to say I'm living,
and that I'm not among the dead.
Though I'm getting more forgetful,
and more mixed up in the head.

Sometimes I can't remember
when I stand at the foot of stair,
if I must go up for something
or if I've just come down from there.

And before the fridge so often
my poor mind is filled with doubt.
Have I just put some food away
or have I come to take some out?

And when it's dark outside sometimes
with my cap upon my head,
I don't know if I'm retiring
or just getting out of bed.

So, if it's my turn to write to you
there's no need in getting sore.
I may think that I've written
and don't want to be a bore.

So, remember, I do love you
and wish that you were here.
But now it's nearly mail time
so, I'll say "goodbye" my dear.

Then I stood beside the mailbox, with a face so red.
Instead of mailing you my letter – I had opened it instead.
XxCamyxX

Shirley Ford

•

PAUL'S GIRL

Paul's girl is rich and haughty.
My girl is poor as clay.
Paul's girl has a nice figure.
My girl is like a bale of hay.
Paul's girl is very smart.
My girl is dumb, but good.
Would I trade places with Paul?
You bet your life I would!
1999 Student Berean Bible Church

•

Since it's the early worm that gets eaten by the bird, sleep late.
Annette Holland

•

The second mouse gets the cheese.
Author Unknown

•

If you lend someone $30
and never see that person again,
it was probably worth it.
Anonymous

•

THE ELECTRICIAN

Somebody said that it couldn't be done
but he, with a smile, replied
that maybe it couldn't, but he would be one
who wouldn't say so 'tll he tried.

So, he buckled right in with a bit of a grin
when his screwdriver touched a live wire.
He let out a cry and proceeded to die
in a shower of sparks and fire.

The people who gave the eulogy
spoke of honor, and love, and ambition.
They spoke well of the dead, and nobody said,
"Why didn't he call an electrician?"
Edgar Albert Guest

•

If you think you are too small to be effective,
you have never been in the dark with a mosquito.
Wolfgang Reibeu

•

Never go to a doctor whose office plants have died.
Erma Bombeck

•

Always keep your words soft and sweet,
just in case you have to eat them.
Andy Rooney

•

Shirley Ford

•

Well, you know what they say: If you don't have
anything nice to say about anybody – come sit by me.
Clairee Belcher

•

Humor is the hook on which we hang our memories.
Author Unknown

•

Sometimes, someone unexpected comes into your life out of
nowhere, makes your heart race, and changes you forever.
We call them traffic cops.
Bizware Magic

•

If you're sitting in public and a stranger takes the seat
next to you, just stare straight ahead and say,
"Did you bring the money?"
The Common Constitutionalist

•

A smile is an inexpensive way to improve your looks.
Andy Rooney

•

Butterflies Are Free

 # ENCOURAGEMENT

STEPS TO A SIMPLE LIFE

When you wake up each day, complete the following statement: "My purpose is to ……………today."

Remember you are too blessed to be stressed.

Always take time to write a thank-you note – no matter how long it's been since the person took their time to remember you.

Meditate for at least 10 minutes each day.

Drink green tea, plenty of water, and eat more vegetables and fruits. Try to make at least three people smile today.

Don't waste your energy on gossip, energy vampires, negative thoughts or things you can't control.

Life isn't fair, but it is still good.

Don't take yourself so seriously. No one else does.

Make peace with your past so it won't spoil the present.

Don't compare your life with others. You have no idea what their journey is about.

No one is in charge of your happiness except you.

Forgive everyone for everything.

What other people think of you is none of your business.

God heals everything.

Your job won't take care of you when you are sick. Your friends will. Stay in touch.

Envy is a waste of time. You already have all you need.

Before you go to bed, complete these statements:
    "I'm thankful for . . . .",
    "Today I accomplished.. . . . ."
Author Unknown

●

Be the person who breaks the cycle.
If you were judged, choose understanding.
If you were rejected, choose acceptance.
If you were shamed, choose compassion.
Be the person you needed when you
were hurting, not the person who hurt you.
Vow to be better than what broke you.
To heal instead of becoming bitter,
so you can act from your heart, not your pain.
Lori Deschene

●

THE GARDEN

I once had a garden filled with flowers
that grew only on dark thoughts.
But they needed my constant attention.
One day I decided I had better things to do.
Brian Andreas

●

THE ANVIL OF GOD'S WORD

Last eve I stood before a blacksmith's door
and heard the anvil ring the vesper chime.
And, looking in, I saw upon the floor
old hammers worn with beating years of time.
"How many anvils have you had," said I,
to wear and batter all the hammers so?"
"Just one," said he, and then with twinkling eye,
"The anvil wears the hammers out, you know."
And so, thought I, the anvil of God's Word
for skeptics' blows have beat upon.
Yet, though the noise of falling blows was heard,
the anvil is unchanged – the hammers gone.
John Clifford

•

TRIALS

Trials must and will befall
but, with humble faith,
to see love inscribed upon them all –
this is happiness to me.

Trials make the promise sweet.
Trials give new life to prayer.
Trials bring me to His feet,
lay me low and keep me there.
William Cowper

•

Shirley Ford

•

CAN YOU HONESTLY JUDGE?

Pray don't find fault with the man
who limps or stumbles along the road,
unless you have worn the shoes he wears
or struggled beneath his load.
There may be tacks in his shoes that hurt,
though hidden from view,
or the burden he bears placed on your back
might cause you to stumble too.
Don't sneer at the man who's down today
unless you have felt the blow that caused the fall
or felt the shame that only the fallen know.
You may be strong, but still the blows that were his
if dealt to you in the self-same way
at the very same time might cause you to stagger too.
Don't be too harsh with the man who sins
or pelt him with words or stones
unless you are sure, yes – doubly sure,
that you have no sins of your own.
Anonymous Philosopher

•

NEVER GIVE UP

Many of life's failures
are people who did not realize
how close they were to success
when they gave up.
Thomas Alva Edison

•

STATE OF MIND

If you think you are beaten – you are.
If you think you dare not – you don't.
If you'd like to win, but feel you can't,
it's almost a cinch that you won't.
If you think you'll lose – you've lost,
for out in the world, you will find
success begins with a fellow's will.
It's all in the state of mind.

Yes, many a game is lost before a play is run.
And many a coward fails before his work is begun.
Think big, and your deeds will grow.
Think small, and you'll fall behind.
Think that you can, and you will.
It's all in the state of mind.

If you think you're outclassed – you are.
You've got to think high to rise.
You've got to be sure of yourself
before you can ever win the prize.
Life's battles don't always go
to the stronger or faster man.
But sooner or later the man who wins
is the fellow who knows he can.
Walter D. Wintle

●

There are two things we get every day.
A chance and a choice
MindfulChristianity

●

Shirley Ford

•

GO FORWARD

With steadfast heart and true
go forward on your way.
God gives you strength to do
the duties of each day.
So daily may this thought
your heart with courage fill,
"I can because I ought,
and by God's help, I will."
Anonymous

•

THE ENEMY

An enemy I had whose face
I stoutly strove to know.
For he had dogged my steps
unseen wherever I did go.

My plans he balked; my aims he failed.
He blocked my onward way.
When some lofty goal I toiled,
he grimly said to me, "nay."

One night I seized and held him fast,
from him the veil did draw.
I looked upon his face at last,
and, lo – myself I saw.
Anonymous

•

THREE THINGS

Three things there are
that will never come back.
The arrow shot forth
on its destined track.
The appointed hour
that could not wait,
and the helpful word
that was spoken too late.
Adapted from the Persian - By Louis Untermeyer

●

IT MIGHT

You never know when someone
might catch a dream from you.
Or something you say may open the
windows of a mind that seeks the light.
The way you live may not matter at all,
but you never know – it might.

And just in case it could be
that another's life, through you,
might possibly change for the better
with a better and brighter view.
It seems it might be worth a try
at pointing the way to the right.
Of course, it may not matter at all,
but then again – it might.
John Clemmeu

●

Shirley Ford

•

ATTITUDE

I believe the single most significant decision
I can make on a day-to-day basis
is my choice of attitude.

It is more important than my past, my education,
my bankroll, my successes or failures,
fame or pain, what other people think of me
or say about me, my circumstances, or my position.

Attitude keeps me going or cripples my progress.
It alone fuels my fire or assaults my hope.
When my attitudes are right there is no barrier too high,
no valley too deep, no dream too extreme,
or no challenge too great for me.
Charles Swindoll

•

SHIPS

There are good ships and wood ships,
and ships that sail the sea,
but the best ships are friendships!
May they always be.
Irish Proverb

•

LIFE

Life is an opportunity - benefit from it.
Life is beauty - admire it.
Life is a dream - realize it.
Life is a challenge – meet it.
Life is duty – complete it.
Life is a game – play it.
Life is a promise – fulfill it.
Life is sorrow – overcome it.
Life is a song – sing it.
Life is a struggle – accept it.
Life is a tragedy – confront it.
Life is an adventure – dare it.
Life is luck – make it.
Life is too precious – do not destroy it.
Life is life – fight for it.
Mother Teresa

●

A MORNING PRAYER

Go with me, Dear Father,
through the coming day.
Keep my lips from speaking
words they should not say.
Guide my hands, Dear Father,
in the work they find.
Teach me to be helpful,
help me to be kind.
Anonymous

Shirley Ford

•

HOPE

"I find I'm so excited I can barely sit still
or hold a thought in my head.
I think it's the excitement only a free man can feel.
A free man at the start of a long journey
whose conclusion is uncertain.
I hope I can make it across the border.
I hope to see my friend and shake his hand.
I hope the Pacific is as blue as in my dreams."
"I hope."
*Red's comments while riding on the bus
at the end of "The Shawshank Redemption."*

•

IT ALL MATTERS

There are no inconsequential moments.
There are no chance encounters.
There are no irrelevant people.
There are no insignificant tasks.
Anonymous
Acts 4:36-37 NASB
(Be a "Barnabas" for someone today.)

•

If you feel like you're losing everything,
remember trees lose their leaves every year yet
they still stand tall and wait for better days to come.
Japanese Legend

•

LIFE'S JOURNEY

How far you go in life depends on
your being tender with the young,
compassionate with the aged,
sympathetic with the striving,
and tolerant of the weak and strong,
because someday in your life
you will have been all of these.

•

OUTWITTED

He drew a circle that shut me out –
heretic, rebel, a thing to flout.
But love and I had the will to win.
We drew a circle that took him in!
Edwin Markham

•

BELIEVE IN YOURSELF

Believe in yourself and what you can do.
Believe in your goals that you strive to pursue.
Believe in your friends who believe in you too.
Forever and always, believe in you.
Anonymous

•

Shirley Ford

•

DIVINE REFUGE

When you accept the fact that sometimes
seasons are dry and times are hard and
that God is in control of both, you will discover a
sense of divine refuge, because the hope
then is in God and not in yourself.
Charles Swindoll

•

PREPARE

For all your days prepare
and meet them ever alike.
When you are the anvil – bear.
When you are the hammer - strike.
Edwin Markham

•

THE SMILE

It was only a sunny smile,
and little it cost in the giving.
But like morning light
it scattered the night
and made the day worth living.
F. Scott Fitzgerald

•

Butterflies Are Free

•

THE BEND IN THE ROAD

Sometimes we come to life's crossroads
and view what we think is the end.
But God had a much wider vision
and He knows it's only a bend.

The road will go on and get smoother,
and after we've stopped for a rest,
the path that lies hidden beyond us
is often the path that is best.

So, rest and relax and grow stronger.
Let go and let God share your load.
Have faith in a brighter tomorrow.
You've just come to a bend in the road.
Helen Steiner Rice

•

COWBOY ETHICS

Live each day with courage.
Take pride in your work.
Always finish what you start.
Do what has to be done.
Be tough, but fair.
When you make a promise – keep it.
Ride for the brand.
Talk less and say more.
Remember that some things aren't for sale.
Know where to draw the line.
James P. Owen
Center For Cowboy Ethics and Leadership

•

PLANS

One does not plan and then try to make
circumstances fit those plans.
One tries to make plans fit the circumstances.
I think the difference between success and failure
depends upon the ability, or lack of it, to do just that.
General George Patton

•

LOAN YOUR MAP

You can't heal the people you love.
You can't make choices for them.
You can't rescue them.

You can promise that they won't journey alone.
You can loan them your map,
but the trip is theirs.
Laura Jean Truman

•

RESPONSIBILITY

We live in a world in which we need to share
responsibility. It's easy to say, "It's not my child,
not my community, not my problem."
Then there are those who see the need and respond.
I consider those people my heroes.
Fred Rogers

•

•

THE JOURNEY

Maybe the journey isn't so much about becoming anything.
Maybe it's about unbecoming everything that isn't you so
that you can be who you were meant to be in the first place.
Charles Swindoll

•

WHEN THEY CAME

When the Nazi's came for the communists,
I remained silent.
I was not a communist.

When they locked up the social democrats,
I remained silent.
I was not a social democrat.

When they came for the trade unionists,
I did not speak out.
I was not a trade unionist.

When they came for the Jews,
I did not speak out.
I was not a Jew.

When they came for me,
There was no one left to speak out.
Friedrich Gustav Martin Niemoller

•

Shirley Ford

●

WHAT IS CHARITY?

It is silence – when your words would hurt.
It is patience - when your neighbor is curt.
It is deafness - when a scandal flows.
It is thoughtfulness - for others' woes.
It is promptness - when duty calls.
It is courage - when misfortune falls.
Author Unknown

●

YOU DECIDE

You have brains in your head.
You have feet in your shoes.
You can steer yourself in any direction you choose.
You are on your own, and you know what you know.
And you are the one who'll decide where to go.
Oh, The Places You'll go! - Dr. Seuss

●

FACING FEAR

Fear has two meanings.
Forget everything and run,
or face everything and rise.
The choice is yours.
Zig Ziglar

●

•

When God puts love and compassion
in your heart toward someone,
He's offering you an opportunity to
make a difference in that person's life.
You must learn to follow that love.
Don't ignore it. Act on it.
Somebody needs what you have.
Joel Osteen

•

Love yourself, accept yourself,
forgive yourself and be good to yourself.
Because without you the rest of us are
without a source of many wonderful things.
Leo Buscaglia

•

BEFORE YOU GET OUT OF BED

Five things to do before you get out of bed –
Express gratitude.
Set your intentions for the day.
Take five long, deep breaths in and out.
Smile for no reason.
Forgive yourself for yesterday's mistakes.
Paul Lenda

•

Shirley Ford

•

OUR DEEPEST FEAR

Our deepest fear is not that we are inadequate.
Our deepest fear is that we are powerful beyond measure.
It is our light, not our darkness, that most frightens us.
We ask ourselves –
Who am I to be brilliant, gorgeous, talented, fabulous?
Actually, who are you not to be? You are a child of God.

Your playing small does not serve the world.
There's nothing enlightened about shrinking
so that other people won't feel insecure around you.

We are all meant to shine, as children do.
We are born to make manifest the
glory of God that is within us.
It's not just in some of us.   It's in everyone.

And as we let our own light shine,
we unconsciously give other people
permission to do the same.
As we're liberated from our own fear,
our presence automatically liberates others.
Marianne Williamson

•

ONENESS

In some way, shape or form, it's what
every person I've met has been seeking.
Phil Knight

•

●

HE WHO KNOWS

He who knows not and knows not that he
knows not is a fool - shun him.
He who knows not and knows that he
knows not is a child – teach him.
He who knows and knows not that he
knows is asleep – wake him.
He who knows and knows that he
knows is wise – follow him.
Persian Proverb

●

STAY YOUNG AND USEFUL ALL YOUR LIFE

Keep learning – especially God's word.
Keep loving.
Keep laughing.
Keep leaving your cares behind.
Keep longing – dreaming.
Change your attitude.
You can do anything you are called to do.
You are young and useful at any age,
If you are still planning for tomorrow.
Keep looking.
Keep laboring.
Keep listening.
Anonymous

●

Shirley Ford

•

ONE PAIR OF HANDS

One pair of hands formed the mountain.
One pair of hands formed the sea.
One pair of hands made the sun and moon,
every bird, every flower, every tree.

One pair of hands formed the valleys,
the ocean, the rivers, and the sand.
Those hands are so strong so when life goes
wrong, put your faith into one pair of hands.

One pair of hands healed the sick.
One pair of hands raised the dead.
One pair of hands calmed the raging storm,
and thousands of people were fed.

One pair of hands said, "I love you,"
and those hands were nailed to a tree.
Those hands are so strong, so when life goes
wrong, put your faith into one pair of hands.
Carroll Roberson

•

You cannot run away from a weakness.
You must sometime fight it out or perish.
And if that be so, why not now – and where you stand?
Robert Louis Stevenson

•

SOWING AND REAPING

Sow a thought, reap an act.
Sow an act, reap a habit.
Sow a habit, reap a character.
Sow a character, reap your destiny.
Ralph Waldo Emerson

●

FAITH

Faith is the song of springtime
that helps us through winter's storms.
Faith is the sunshine we remember
throughout the darkest hours of night.
Faith gives strength to our hearts
when we need it the most.
Faith gives us hope for tomorrow.
Annonymous

●

TAKE TIME

Take time to work – it is the price of success.
Take time to think – it is the source of power.
Take time to play – it is the secret of perpetual youth.
Take time to read – it is the fountain of wisdom.
Take time to be friendly – it is the road to happiness.
Take time to dream - it is hitching your wagon to a star.
Take time to love and to be loved – it is the privilege of the gods.
Take time to look around – it is too short a day to be selfish.
Take time to laugh – it is the music of the soul.
Old English Prayer

●

●

Everyone wants to live on top of the mountain,
but all the happiness and growth occur
while you're climbing it.
Andy Rooney

●

Never allow someone to be your priority
while allowing yourself to be their option.
Mark Twain

●

At times, our own light goes out and is rekindled
by a spark from another person. Each of us has
cause to think with deep gratitude of those
who have lighted the flame within us.
Albert Schweitzer

●

10 THINGS THAT REQUIRE ZERO TALENT

Being on time.
Making an effort.
Being high energy.
Having a positive attitude.
Being passionate.
Using good body language.
Being coachable.
Doing a little extra.
Being prepared.
Having a strong work ethic.
Tim Gimbel

●

THE POWER OF WORDS

A careless word may kindle strife.
A cruel work may wreck a life.
A bitter word may hate instill.
A brutal word may smite and kill.
Pearls From Many Seas, T. J. Bach

•

WISE WORDS

Don't undermine your worth by comparing yourself with others.
It is because we are different that each of us is special.

Do not set your goals by what other people deem important.
Only God knows what is best for you.

Do not take for granted the things closest to your heart.
Cling to them as you would your life,
for without them life is meaningless.

Do not let your life slip through your fingers
by living in the past nor for the future.
By living your life one day at a time,
you live all the days of your life.

Do not give up when you still have something to give.
Nothing is really over until the moment you stop trying.

Do not be afraid to encounter risks.
It is by taking chances that we learn how to be brave.

Do not shut love out of your life by saying it is impossible to find.
The quickest way to receive love is to give love.
The fastest way to lose love is to hold it too tightly.

Do not dismiss your dreams.
To be without dreams is to be without hope.
To be without hope is to be without purpose.

Do not run through life so fast that you forget not only
where you have been, but also where you are going.

Life is not a race, but a journey
to be savored each step of the way.
Anonymous

•

THE MAN IN THE GLASS

When you get what you want in your struggle for
self and the world makes you king for a day,
just go to the mirror and look at yourself
and see what that man has to say.

For it isn't your father, or mother, or wife,
whose judgement upon you must pass.
The fellow whose verdict counts most in your
life is the one staring back from the glass.

He's the fellow to please – never mind all the rest.
For he's with you, clear to the end, and you've passed
your most difficult dangerous test if the
man in the glass is your friend.

You may fool the whole world down the pathway
of years and get pats on the back as you pass.
But the final reward will be heartache and tears,
if you've cheated the man in the glass.
Peter Dale Wimdrow, Sr.

•

Butterflies Are Free

Shirley Ford

 # THE CHILDREN'S HOUR

THE FIRST LESSON

Raise your child so that he will make
himself do what he knows has to be done,
when it should be done, whether he likes it or not.
It is the first lesson that ought to be learned,
and however early a man's training begins,
it is probably the last lesson he learns thoroughly.
Henry David Thoreau

●

A HANDPRINT

Sometimes you get discouraged
because I am so small,
and always leave my fingerprints
on furniture and wall.

But everyday I'm growing,
I'll be grown up some day
and all those tiny fingerprints
will surely fade away.

So, here's a final handprint
just so you can recall
exactly how my fingers looked
when I was very small.
Drew Magary, The Hike

●

Shirley Ford

•

HUMAN NATURE

You don't really understand human nature unless
you know why a child on a merry-go-round
will wave at his parents every time he
goes around . . . . . . and why his parents
will always wave back!
Anonymous

•

You should never say no to a gift from a child.
Andy Rooney

•

SOMEDAY

Someday I'll sit and reminisce
of harried, hectic days like this.
I'll rock and knit and hanker for
some muddy footprints on my floor.
For a cookie jar that's always bare
and playthings scattered everywhere.
For childish voices, shrill and thin,
'til one can't think above the din.
In lonely yearning I'll recall
the finger smudges on my wall.
But, please, won't someone tell me how
I'm ever going to stand it now?
Olive Jensen

•

THE TEACHER

I want to teach my students how
to live a life on this earth.
To face it's struggles and its strife
and to improve their worth.
Not just a lesson in a book
or how the rivers flow,
but how to choose the proper path
wherever they may go.
To understand eternal truth
and know the right from wrong.
To gather all the beauty
of a flower and a song.
For if I help the world to grow
in wisdom and in grace,
then I shall feel that I have won
and I have filled my place.
And so I ask for guidance, God,
that I may do my part
for character and confidence
and happiness of heart.
James J. Metcalf

•

Simple walks with my father around the block
on summer nights when I was a child
did wonders for me as an adult.
Andy Rooney

•

Shirley Ford

•

A PIECE OF CLAY

I took a piece of waxing clay
and idly fashioned it one day.
And as my fingers pressed it still,
it moved and yielded to my will.

I came again when days were past –
the bit of clay was hard at last.
The form I gave it, it still bore,
but I could change that form no more.

I took a piece of living clay
and gently formed it day-by-day.
And molded with my power and art,
a young child's soft and yielding heart.

I came again when years were gone –
it was a man I looked upon.
He still that early impress wore,
and I could change him never more.
Anonymous

•

Pick it up, pick it up,
put it on the shelf.
Don't leave it for Mother
but pick it up yourself!
A childrens' song from the "Happy Hank Radio Show."
A radio version of television's Mr. Rogers Neighborhood.
It was created by Marc Williams and aired in the 1940's.

•

REFLECTIONS

My mind drifts back to childhood years
when you would hold me near
and heal my sometimes-wounded heart
and calm my every fear.

I remember you were there for me.
I knew that I belonged.
In my eyes you were so handsome
and, oh, so very strong.

I look back and I realize
just how much we shared.
Though I thought your rules too tough,
you were always very fair.

I'm grown now, Dad,
and, oh, the love now easy to relay,
is measured by our cherished talks
we have from day-to-day.

Forever you have stood by me.
On you I can depend.
Now there's no one in this world
I'd rather call my friend.
Author Unknown

I ASK

I ask Thee for a sure and certain skill,
a patient and a consecrated will.
I ask Thee for a white and perfect dream;
a vision of the deep and wide unseen.

I ask Thee for a love that understands
when it should reach and when withdraw its hands.
A selflessness that flings the locked door wide
for youth to enter while I step aside.
Dear Lord, I need these things so much – so much.
a human soul lies plastic to my touch!
Author Unknown

•

HE'S JUST A LITTLE BOY

He stands at the plate with his heart pounding fast.
The bases are loaded, the die has been cast.
Mom and Dad cannot help him, he stands all alone.
A hit at the moment would send the team home.

The ball meets the plate, he swings and misses.
There's a groan from the crowd, with some boos and hisses.
A thoughtless voice shouts, "Throw out the bum."
Tears fill his eyes – the game is no longer fun.

So, open your heart and give him a break,
for it's the memories like this a man you can make.
Keep this in mind when you hear someone forget:
He's just a little boy, and not a man yet.
Bluestone Dam Community Park
Hinton, West Virginia - 1999

•

THE THINGS SHE TOOK

Most often when we think of Mom
we think of all she's given.
The softness of a loving touch,
a gentle guide for living.
A nightly tiptoe in the room,
an understanding look.
But sometimes, when I think of Mom,
I think of all she took.
She took a child and taught it how
to live a life with pride.
She took those kindergarten tears,
and kept them all inside.
She took the hands that longed
to hold her child and not let go.
Used them to push her child
along the way to thrive and grow.
Took time to do some other things,
like sew, and clean, and cook.
And never thought to ask for thanks
for all the things she took.
Anonymous

Shirley Ford

•

ANGELS BY YOUR BED TONIGHT

Darkness covers all the land – sounds of day are gone;
but love is all around you now and will be 'til the dawn.

Stars shine on the window sill, the moon shines
through the trees; angels by your bed
tonight – shine where no one sees.

So there's no need to be afraid all the whole night
through, 'cause God has made a promise child,
that He'll take care of you.

All that you've been dreamin' of awaits you
when you rise; so, with the peace that Jesus brings,
close your sleepy eyes.
Don Francisco

•

LOVE AT HOME

Love wipes away the tears
before it wipes up the spilled milk.

Love smiles at the tiny fingerprints
on a newly-cleaned window.

Love is present through the trials.

Love reprimands, reproves, and is responsive.

Love leaves the dust in search of a child's laugh.
Author Unknown

•

THE WATCHER

She always leaned to watch for us,
anxious if we were late.
In winter by the window;
in summer by the gate.

And though we mocked her tenderly
who had such foolish care,
the long way home would seem more
safe because she waited there.

Her thoughts were all full of us;
she never could forget.
And so I think that where she is
she must be watching yet.

Waiting 'til we come home to her;
anxious if we are late.
Watching from heaven's window;
leaning from heaven's gate.
Margaret Widdemer

Shirley Ford

•

IF I HAD MY CHILD TO RAISE OVER AGAIN

If I had my child to raise over again,
I'd finger paint more and point the finger less.
I'd do less correcting, and more connecting.
I'd take my eyes off the watch,
and watch with my eyes.
I would care to know less and know to care more.
I'd take more hikes and fly more kites.
I'd stop playing serious, and seriously play.
I'd run through more fields,
and gaze at more stars.
I'd do more hugging, and less tugging.
I would be firm less often and affirm much more.
I'd build self-esteem first, and the house later.
I'd teach less about the love of power,
and more about the power of love.
It matters not whether my child is big or small,
from this day forth, I'll cherish it all.
Diana Loomans

•

Butterflies Are Free

Shirley Ford

 SOME STORIES

LIFE'S SNOW GLOBES

It was the last day of the year and business was humming at the restaurant with customers who had been shopping for year-end bargains at the local mall. Mothers and their small children rested their tired feet while having a bite to eat and happily share their plans to celebrate the "ringing in of the New Year" that evening.

He was a cute little three-year-old with a headful of blond curls. In his little hands he held a small snow globe which made the sparkling snow swirl around the colorful figure inside whenever he shook it. Excitedly, he shared it with me - his favorite Christmas toy that he carried with him everywhere. I thanked him for sharing it with me and then continued on my way to the other customers.

Suddenly there was a crash, the sound of breaking glass, a scream, and uncontrollable sobbing. The snow globe had slipped from the small hands and now lay shattered in a million tiny pieces on the cold, gray, tile floor. At that moment, nothing would console the little boy with the blond curls. His much-loved snow globe was gone!

As I swept up the pieces, I thought of times in life when each of us have had our "snow globes" shattered and screamed out – "WHY?". What happened? One minute things are going along okay, and the next everything is turned upside down.

Life has a way of suddenly changing directions for each of us. It's in those moments we find out where our real strengths lie. It's where our faith can grow. We can try to take control, or we can step back and let faith show us a new path.

The first steps are scary and rocky at first, but it can be exciting to see a new direction – one that takes us to places we never imagined we were capable of traveling to. Which direction will we choose?

Faith does not grow in a house of certainty.
William Paul Young

Proverbs 3:5-6 NASB

●

LISTEN AND SILENT

Maybe this is something to think about for a few minutes.

It takes the same six letters to spell the words "listen" and "silent" – they are just in a different order.

Do you ever have a problem with just quietly listening to what someone is telling you and not be thinking of your response to their story before they finish? I'm guilty! And sometimes, rudely, start talking while they are still talking. You'd think I would do better, as I know how it feels when it happens to me.

The most powerful way to heal someone is to listen. Don't think or judge. Just listen. People start to heal the moment they feel they are being heard. You can't be a healer if you refuse to step outside of your own emotions and view things entirely from the perspective of another person.

James 1:19 NASB

●

THE RESTAURANT

She came home to the dark, empty, house after a long day at work. She was tired. She thought about supper and, although she wasn't hungry, believed it would be good to find something to eat – maybe at a restaurant where there would be other people.

It had been too many years for her to remember when the last time it was that she had gone out to eat supper by herself. Mealtime was always a time when you heard how everyone's day had been. You listened and shared the ups and down's, laughed (and sometimes there were tears), and shared plans for the tomorrows.

Her life was so strange now – completely changed from the happy, routine days before she lost her husband of almost 50 years. He was her best friend and encourager. He always told her she could do anything she set out to do. Over the years, she had come to depend on his support and input into her "adventures." But tonight, that was gone. The only thing she felt was loneliness, fear, and weakness.

She remembered that a new little restaurant had just opened in the nearby shopping center. Why not give it a try? It might not be too busy with customers, and it was easy to drive to.

After parking the car, she got out and walked to the restaurant. With a crossword-puzzle book clutched in her hand for something to distract her (today we rely on our cell phones), she took a deep breath, pulled open the door and stepped inside. She felt everyone had stopped what they were doing and turned to see who had just walked in.

In her mind, the place was packed. To be honest, there were only a half-dozen customers who were just enjoying each other's company and really didn't see her walk in.

The young waitress came to her and told her she could sit wherever she would like. The counter at the large front window overlooking the busy shopping center's parking lot seemed like a safe place. As she sat on the stool watching the shoppers and cars come and go outside, it took her mind off herself and gave her a small amount of peace.

For a first try, the evening went as well as it could. The scared feeling was still there but she had managed to eat the hamburger and fries and then head home to the quiet house.

It was now the end of September. The leaves were starting to change their colors to the brilliant shades of orange, red, and yellow. Signs of Fall were all around, brought on by the nice warm days and cool nights. She continued her routine of going to the restaurant for supper on her way home from work.

Business was slow so there was time to visit with the owners. They had moved to the area from New York with a plan to open their own restaurant. He had enjoyed working as a chef in a popular restaurant back home. They were excited about the opportunity for them to pursue their dream.

A couple of months went by bringing the short, dark days of Winter. It was getting a little easier to open the door and walk into the restaurant. She still held on to the puzzle book, just in case she would need a distraction.

People everywhere were starting to make plans for the holidays. Thanksgiving, Christmas and New Year's Day were fast approaching. Invitations came to dinners and holiday events, changing her evening routine. She only went to the restaurant a few times during November and December.

By now the holidays had come and gone and a new year was beginning. She decided to go back to see how the couple and their business were doing. When she pulled into the parking lot, she was not ready for what she saw. The restaurant was dark – no welcoming lights anywhere. A, "Closed – Property for Sale", sign was posted on the plate-glass window where she had sat keeping vigil – where she slowly had found courage to move ahead and face her fears.

What had happened? Where did they go? For the next few weeks, she asked employees in neighboring businesses if they knew why the business had closed. The answer was always the same: "Too busy with the holidays and really never had the time to pay attention or talk with the owners."

For her, they had been a gift – "A very present help in time of need." The restaurant and the owners had provided a haven for her to come to peace with her fears and restore a degree of her self-confidence.

Wherever they are, she continues to pray that the couple have found their dream and are doing well. She owes them so much for the kindness and friendship they gave to her at a time she needed so much.

Psalm 46:1   NASB

•

Shirley Ford

•

AN HOUR OF SILENCE – WHAT WOULD YOU PAY?

The radio talk-show host said that now a company was selling "An Hour of Complete Silence" to anyone who was willing to pay their fee.

Wow! My first thought was it is just another great way to sell a product to an already fad-oriented public. As I dressed for the day and then went to a local coffee shop for breakfast on my way to work, the hosts words wouldn't go away. What are we doing to ourselves, and where is the quiet place today?

Instead of reading the newspaper as I usually did, I watched the customers as they went through the line. The majority were talking on their cell phone or texting with someone. Many were teenagers who were continually in animated motion. As this was 7:30 a.m. on a school day, I wondered what their schedule could be.

I looked out the window and saw customers scampering across the parking lot to an office supply store, a mailing business, and a grocery store. Each appeared to have an agenda with "Rush" stamped at the very top of the page. I'm just as much a part of this madness as each person I saw this morning.

I was given the opportunity to see if I could change my way of thinking. After a company layoff, I continued to keep a "to do" list of everything I thought I should do. Things were crossed off as I completed each task. But each time I would run an errand, I found people who were enjoying the day and would want to stop and talk with me about the weather, something new they had just noticed in the area – any subject that was important to them. With few exceptions, they would end the conversation about how much they were enjoying the day.

I decided to try removing habits that were in control of me and see if I would experience any changes in my way of thinking. First, I decided to limit the number of programs I always listened to while I was trying to do 12 other things. I found that while I still care deeply about what is happening in and to our country and local events, I think more about the issues and solutions and am less stressed and negative about the "what ifs." To have the media repeat over and over about situations they do not have the complete facts on is only pouring gas on an already red-hot fire.

Someone very wisely suggested that if a person decides to set his own pace each day, it will take at least one year to make the change. How true that is. First, I decided to think before I quickly said "yes" to work, projects, invitations – the way I had always lived. It isn't easy, as old habits are very strong – a daily challenge.

I'll try to listen more and talk less. The best part of listening to someone is hearing the many interesting things you learn when you allow someone else to tell their story.

Cease striving and know that I am God.
Psalm 46:10 NASB

•

WHAT DID HE WRITE?

We really don't know.

The townspeople brought her to Him. They said they had caught her in the act of adultery breaking the law of Moses which carried the penalty of stoning a person to death.

He looked at her - then at her accusers. They were using this to test Him so they would have grounds to accuse Him of breaking the Mosaic law. He stooped and, using His finger, began writing something in the loose earth – saying nothing.

Did He write something that reminded each one of something they knew they themselves to be guilty? Maybe a word like Thief? Liar? Hater? Gossip? Envy? Did their conscience remind them of the sin they each were guilty of hiding in their life?

Standing up and looking at them He said, "He who is without sin be the first to cast a stone." Then He knelt and began to write more words. As they watched Him write, one-by-one each turned and silently walked away leaving Him alone with the accused.

When no one remained but the woman He rose to His feet. "Is there anyone here to accuse you", He asked. When she replied, "No", He told her to go and sin no more.

Ahh, when we point a finger . . . .

John 8:3-11 NASB

•

A CHALLENGE FOR YOU

Do you like challenges – maybe one that is a little scary?

If you ever get the chance, go alone.

    Walk alone.   Travel alone.   Dance alone.

    Just for a while!

When you get the chance, learn who you are when the world isn't demanding you to be one way or another.

When you get the chance, know that the opportunity to walk alone, even for a bit, is a rare gift and one that will hand you insight that changes the course of your life.

    Make friends with the real you!

•

HUMILITY

Ouch!!! Getting a lesson in humility hurts. I thought I was doing great. After all, everyone else was having all the problems with health, teenagers, relationships, household maintenance, etc. Then things started to crumble.

Anything you can name in your life that runs with a battery needed one; from a garage-door opener, a wristwatch, smoke detectors, and everything you can think of in between.

Then not to be left out, the battery in my car died. Now that it had my attention, the water pump went out on the car.

Well, that's when I finally stopped and asked myself if maybe I should have reacted in a better way to people who had shared what was happening to them. Things that were frustrating or hurting them. Things that will take time before they can be resolved. Things that have changed their life forever.

The dead batteries were a friendly reminder to stop, step back, and hear and see what others are going through. Stop and offer a listening ear or a helping hand wherever it is needed.

Don't let your arrogance outrun your ignorance!

•

THE GIFT OF WORDS

"Let no hurtful or foul words come from your mouth. Say only words that are good for encouragement according to the need of the moment, so that it will give grace to those who hear."

Whoa – really? This is huge! Thinking of our words as gifts is a powerful concept. This verse, Ephesians 4:29, tells us that what we choose to say matters.

I ordered an item on Amazon through the internet from a company based in China. Tracking the shipment daily, it took three weeks for it to be packaged, shipped, pass through customs in China, them again when it entered the United States and was repackaged, be accepted by USPS, and then delivered to my home. I was pleased things had gone so well.

Then I went to the local grocery store to purchase an item I needed. When I was unable to find it, I asked the Customer Service employee if they carried the item. She looked it up on her cell phone and said they did not.

Her next words were a reminder to choose my words wisely when I speak to anyone. She looked up at my gray hair and said, "Honey, you can get your grandchildren to order this for you on Amazon."

We can bless someone with our words, or we can tear someone down. We can encourage someone, or deflate them. We have the ability to affirm, or offend.

Are your words a gift? Every time you speak, you get to choose the words that come from your lips.

Will you choose wisely?

•

HAPPINESS

We convince ourselves that life will be better once we graduate from school, get that job, marry, have a family.

Then we get frustrated with our small children and believe that all will be well when they are older. We find adolescence a challenge to deal with. Surely, we'll be happier when they grow out of the teen years.

We tell ourselves our life will be better when we have a nicer car. When we have a nicer house. When we can take a vacation. When we finally retire.

The truth is there is no better time to be happy than right now. If not, then when? Your life will always be full of challenges. It is better to admit as much and decide to be happy in spite of it all.

For a long time it seems that life is about to start. Real life. But there are always obstacles along the way. A challenge to work through. Some work that needs to be finished. Time to be given to a someone who needs help. Bills that need to be paid. Then life will start. We finally come to the understanding that those obstacles are life.

That point of view helps us see that there isn't any road to happiness. Happiness is the road.

So, enjoy every moment. Stop waiting for school to end, to lose ten pounds, for work to begin, to get married, for Friday evening, for Sunday morning, waiting for a new car, for your mortgage to be paid off, for Spring, for Summer, for Fall, for Winter, for the first or the fifteenth of the month, for your song to be played on the radio, to die, to be reborn . . . . . . before deciding to be happy.

>   Happiness is a voyage, not a destination.
>   There is no better time to be happy than now.
>   Live and enjoy the moment.

•

PASS IT ON

Try to answer these questions:
- Name the 3 richest people in the world.
- Name the last 3 Miss America winners.
- Name the last 3 Nobel Prize winners.

Can't do it? A little difficult?   Don't worry, nobody remembers the answers. Applause dies away! Trophies gather dust! Winners are soon forgotten.

Now try to answer these questions:
- Name 3 teachers who contributed to your education.
- Name 3 friends who helped you in your hour of need.
- Name 3 people that you like to spend time with.

Butterflies Are Free

It's easier, isn't it? The people who mean something in your life are not rated as "the best", or have the most money, and haven't won the greatest prizes. They are the ones who care about you. Support you. Those who, no matter what, stay close by.

Think about it for a moment. Life is very short! And you, in which list are you? Don't know? Let me give you a hand. You are not among the most "famous", but among friends who remember.

A few years ago at the Seattle Special Olympics, nine mentally or physically challenged athletes were standing at the start line for the 100-meter race. The gun fired and the race began. Each one participating was struggling to win. A boy tripped and fell and started crying. The others slowed down to see what had happened. Then they stopped and came back . . . ALL OF THEM!

The girl with Down's Syndrome sat down next to him, hugged him, and asked, "Feel better now?" Then ALL nine walked shoulder-to-shoulder to the finish line. The whole crowd stood up and applauded. And the applause continued for a very long time.

People who witnessed this still talk about it. Why? Because deep down inside each of us, we know that the most important thing in life is much more than winning for ourselves. The most important thing in this life is to help others to win. Even if that means slowing down and changing our own race.

If we pass this message on perhaps we will succeed in changing not only our hearts but someone else's heart as well.

A candle loses nothing when it lights another candle.
Thomas Jefferson
Based on an event which actually took place at the 1976 Special Olympics in Seattle, Washington.

•

IT'S NOT OVER

He stopped at the table where I was sitting eating my breakfast and, hesitantly, he asked if he could ask me a question. He is a "regular" in the restaurant, and we have had some pleasant conversations over the years – nothing serious. This time his facial expression showed something was weighing heavy on his mind.

I said it was no problem and was surprised by his reply. "Did I find that days now seemed to be long and somewhat strange with retirement. Had people ask me when was I going to retire and what did I plan to do when I did retire while I was still working? Did that bother me? Did I look back and think of things I did when I was 20, or 40, or 60, and see how fast time slipped away but now it crept along? Why did I choose to work now when others were electing not to and wondered why I would work?" I respected his questions, and we had a good discussion.

The rest of the day I kept thinking about his comments - a slice of life you keep in the back of your mind because you don't know how to be honest with yourself. Then a thought surfaced – aren't these the same questions we were asked by well-meaning friends and relatives when we were 20? And 40? And 60? What were our plans for the future? What job did we want to pursue? And why would we want to do that? Maybe it was in real concern for us, just nosey, or just to make conversation.

But here we are at the other end of life, and we're re-living and looking for answers to questions we find even harder to answer this time. This time, not everyone is looking for a new path. This time, whatever each person chooses is more singular and lonely because not everyone is looking for this new path.

Maybe we've traded that thick head of brown hair for thinning gray hair (or none). We've traded the ruddy complexion and tight muscles for wrinkles and sagging body parts – BUT IT'S NOT OVER. God hasn't given up on us – and neither should we. We have a story to tell to those behind us that we need to share. We have experience on our side. That trying new adventures is still there for everyone – young and old. We need to find the doors that are waiting for us to open. They are out there. It won't be easy, but the rewards are enormous.

It's not over - until we quit trying!!

•

 **ONE LINERS**

Butterflies Are Free

•

If you say what you think,
Don't expect to hear only what you like.
Graffiti

•

Life is nothing without friendship.
Cicero

•

Too often we underestimate the power of a touch,
a smile, a kind word,
a listening ear, an honest compliment,
or the smallest act of caring,
all of which have the potential to turn a life around.
Leo Buscaglia

•

Don't be dismayed at goodbyes.
A farewell is necessary before you can meet again.
And meeting again, after moments or a lifetime,
is certain for those who are friends.
Richard Bach

•

To forget is good, but hard.
To forgive is better.
Best of all is reconciliation.
Hans von Luck, Panzer
The memoris of Colonel Hans Von Luck

•

Shirley Ford

•

We all love a hug once in a while.
It lets us know we are loved.
Unknown

•

"Remember, Red, hope is a good thing.
Maybe the best of things, and no good thing ever dies."
Andy's letter to Red - "The Shawshank Redemption"

•

Faith does not grow in a house of certainty.
William Paul Young, The Shack

•

With time and patience, the mulberry leaf becomes satin.
Chinese Proverb

•

When you can't control what's happening,
challenge yourself to control the way you
respond to what's happening.
That's where your power is!
Author Unknown

•

You should never give up,
no matter how hard the situation is.
Always believe that something
beautiful is going to happen.
Charles Swindoll

•

Butterflies Are Free

•

I think that when the dust settles,
we will realize how very little we need,
how very much we actually have,
and the true value of human connection.
Tina Buddha

•

Success is not final.
Failure is not fatal.
It's the courage to continue that counts.
Winston Churchill

•

It's never too late to be what you might have been.
George Eliot

•

And the day came when the risk
to remain tight in a bud was more painful
than the risk it took to blossom.
Anais Nin

•

It's not doing the things we like to do,
but liking the things we have to do
that makes life blessed.
Goethe

•

Shirley Ford

•

Kindness is the language which
the deaf can hear
and the blind can see.
Mark Twain

•

It takes the same letters to spell the words *listen* and *silent*.
Rena Perozich

•

The real art of conversation is not only
to say the right thing at the right time,
but also to leave unsaid the wrong thing
at the tempting moment.
Dorothy Nevill

•

The smile on my face doesn't mean my life is perfect. It means
I appreciate what I have and what I have been blessed with.
I choose to be happy.
Author Unknown

•

Worrying won't stop the bad stuff from happening.
It stops you from enjoying the good.
Ben Francis

•

I don't have time to worry about who doesn't like me.
I'm too busy loving the people who do love me.
Tiny Budda – Author Unknown

•

•

Light travels faster than sound.
That's why some people appear bright
until you hear them speak.
Albert Einstein

•

There is all the difference in the world between having
to say something and having something to say!
John Dewey

•

You are never too old to set another goal
or dream a new dream.
C. S. Lewis

•

"I can't find my way out of this hole," said Tiny Dragon.
Big Panda smiled and said,
"Then I will come and sit in it with you."
James Norbury – From Big Panda & Tiny Dragon

•

Hope is the thing with feathers that perches in the soul
and sings the tunes without words and never stops at all.
Emily Dickinson

•

Live in such a way that if someone spoke badly of you,
no one would believe it.
Unknown

•

Shirley Ford

•

"Promise me you'll always remember –
You're braver than you believe,
stronger than you seem,
and smarter than you think."
Christopher Robin to Pooh

•

Life has got a habit of not standing hitched.
You've got to ride it like you find it.
You've got to change with it.
Woody Guthrie

•

If you don't build castles in the air,
you won't build anything on the ground.
Victor Hugo

•

Being kind is more important than being right.
Andy Rooney

•

Do not ask the name of the person
who seeks a bed for the night.
He who Is reluctant to give his name
is the one who most needs shelter.
Victor Hugo

•

Butterflies Are Free

•

Do what you can where you are with what you have.
Don't let what you don't know or have paralyze you.
Theodore Roosevelt

•

Much good work is often lost for lack of a little more.
Edward H. Harriman

•

How lucky I am to have something
that makes saying goodbye so hard.
A. A. Milne

•

Use what talents you possess!
The woods would be very silent if no birds
sang there except those that sang the best.
Henry Van Dyke

•

We could learn a lot from crayons.
Some are sharp, some are pretty, some are dull,
while others are bright, some have weird names,
but they all have to live in the same box.
Robert Fulghum

•

In joined hands there is still some token of hope.
In the clenched fist, none.
Victor Hugo

•

•

Change your opinions – keep to your principles.
Change your leaves – keep intact your roots.
Victor Hugo

•

A promise made is a debt unpaid.
A promise fulfilled is a promise kept.
Robert A. Service, Canadian Poet

•

A lie doesn't become truth.
A wrong doesn't beome right.
And evil doesn't become good
just because it's accepted by a majority.
Booker T. Washington

•

Hope is not a strategy.
Rudy Giuliani

•

A mistake that makes you humble is better
than an achievement that makes you arrogant.
Author Unknown

•

Just because people are fueled by drama
doesn't mean you have to attend the performance.
Cheryl Richardson

•

Two things define you!
Your patience when you have nothing,
and your attitude when you have everything.
Imasm Ali

•

What you do, who you're with, and how you feel
about the world around you is completely up to you.
Mike Rowe

•

Anything worth doing hurts a little.
Mike Rowe

•

Happiness does not come from a job.
It comes from knowing what you truly value,
and behaving in a way that is consistent with those beliefs.
Mike Rowe

•

How are we ever going to accomplish anything
in this Incredibly devisive time if we associate
only with people that we don't disagree with?
Mike Rowe

•

God gives the strongest soldiers the toughest battles.
Author Unknown

•

Shirley Ford

•

If you want to be the best, then you have to do
the things other people are not willing to do.
Michael Phelps

•

It is better to fail in a cause that will ultimately succeed
than to succeed in a cause that will ultimately fail.
Peter Marshall

•

Everyone wants to be the sun,
to lighten up someone's life.
But why not be the moon –
to shine in someone's darkest hour?
Taylor James

•

To be rich is not what you have in your bank account,
but what you have in your heart.
Anonymous

•

I learned a simple lesson about being awesome.
Always play to the size of your heart –
not to the size of your audience.
Jon Acuff

•

Everyone you meet deserves to be greeted with a smile.
Andy Rooney

•

Butterflies Are Free

•

90% perfect and launched always changes more lives than
100% perfect and stuck in your head.
Jon Acuff

•

Don't fail.
Experiment and learn from the things that blow up!
Jon Acuff

•

The only thing you are entitled to is hard work
and the ridiculously awesome results that come from it.
Jon Acuff

•

Opportunities are never lost;
someone will take the ones you miss.
Andy Rooney

•

One of the most cowardly things ordinary people do
is to shut their eyes to facts.
C. S. Lewis

•

The best weight you'll ever lose
is the weight of other people's opinion.
Leslie Bradshaw

•

Shirley Ford

Happiness is a butterfly which when pursued
is always just beyond your grasp,
but which if you will sit down quietly,
may alight upon you.
Nathaniel Hawthorne

Shirley Ford grew up on a farm in Ohio with two sisters and a brother. Experiences shared have provided many good disciplines for life. She has enjoyed living in the Woodstock, Georgia, area for almost fifty years and has a daughter, son, daughter-in-law, and two grandchildren.

www.ingramcontent.com/pod-product-compliance
Lightning Source LLC
LaVergne TN
LVHW021714080426
835510LV00010B/1003